AF812100

PLAYGROUND EDUCATION

CREATED and WRITTEN by

R. TOBIAS PITTMAN

PUGSLEY PANDA

Original Illustrations by
William Chislum

To Robert and Bessie, who taught me the true value of a dollar and the worth of a dream.

The Educational Kidz

Formal Francine
Green Greg
Health Harold
History Hope
Holiday Henry
Kindness Karl
Polite Petunia
Time Terrence

Pugsley Panda

Playground Education
P.O. Box 169
Beverly, MA 01915

pugsleypanda@gmail.com

THE MONEY COMPASS

Your Guide to Earning, Spending, Saving, and Thriving

WORKBOOK

Welcome to Your Financial Future

The world of money can often feel like a puzzle with missing pieces. We are told to "be smart" with our finances, but we aren't always shown the map to get there. That is why **The Money Compass** was created.

This is not a typical textbook. This is a **hands-on workbook** designed to move beyond theory and into **real-world application**. Across these pages, we will break down the complex world of finance into **five essential pillars**: **Earning, Saving, Spending, Growing Wealth, and Giving.**

With over 75 pages of interactive activities, you aren't just reading about money—you are practicing the skills that lead to true independence. Whether you are calculating your first paycheck or building a "Savings Shield," you are holding the tools to navigate your own path.

It's time to find your direction. Let's get to work.

Pugsley Panda

Playground Education

Chapter 1: The Land of Earnings

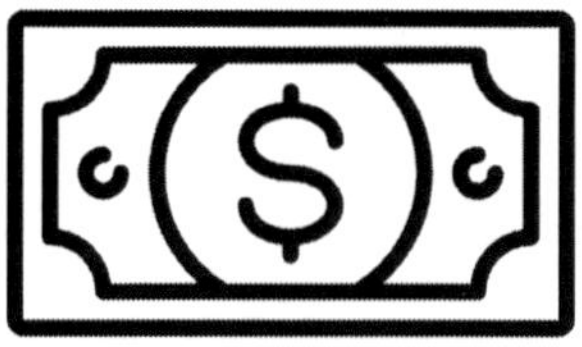

Chapter 2: The Island of Savings

Chapter 3: The Town of Spending

Chapter 4: The Garden of Growing Wealth

Chapter 5: The Grove of Giving

Chapter 1: The Land of Earnings

Ways to earn money

Which of these are ways Clover and you can earn money?
Circle Yes or No

Walking a dog: Yes or No

Playing video games: Yes or No

Selling Lemonade: Yes or No

Sleeping late: Yes or No

Helping with chores: Yes or No

Watching television: Yes or No

Scrolling on social media: Yes or No

Cutting the neighbors yard: Yes or No

Babysitting for neighbors: Yes or No

Tutoring math: Yes or No

Earnings

Find more ways to earn money

Word Search

Q	T	I	M	M	J	L	M	K	T	G	B	S	J	P	I	U	F	L	L
I	D	A	W	Y	E	T	E	Z	Y	U	B	E	U	Q	M	D	Y	H	R
V	T	B	H	K	B	J	T	S	A	K	T	Q	U	O	A	K	L	J	Y
H	M	C	Y	H	N	Y	L	P	R	Z	H	O	J	A	H	O	T	R	N
T	C	A	D	X	C	Z	D	W	D	X	F	Q	R	G	M	W	S	L	W
C	Z	E	C	C	C	C	Q	S	W	M	L	H	G	I	Q	N	Q	L	B
Q	J	V	R	A	V	K	O	P	O	T	K	D	T	A	N	Q	D	G	S
N	I	D	Z	C	H	S	R	N	R	B	I	F	U	M	H	G	D	N	D
N	Y	X	B	C	L	Q	Y	W	K	F	Y	G	C	A	C	C	R	I	N
D	G	U	T	A	J	B	G	Y	I	H	G	L	V	L	G	R	I	L	A
J	O	E	T	W	B	H	Y	R	N	L	N	E	G	L	N	A	P	E	R
B	P	G	I	V	R	Y	R	E	N	O	I	M	N	O	I	F	Q	V	R
J	Q	D	W	I	K	L	S	V	S	D	P	O	I	W	L	T	H	O	E
W	B	Y	T	A	W	X	Q	I	B	W	L	N	K	A	C	S	S	H	Q
F	I	G	I	V	L	O	D	L	T	L	E	A	R	N	Y	E	A	S	N
B	J	H	Y	D	O	K	X	E	J	T	H	D	O	C	C	R	W	I	E
H	H	T	J	I	L	I	J	D	J	Z	I	E	W	E	E	O	R	S	S
C	L	E	A	N	I	N	G	P	N	U	Q	N	Y	F	R	H	A	V	D
T	U	R	N	Y	V	D	P	U	V	Z	M	Y	G	I	F	C	C	O	B
D	M	Q	O	Z	B	J	G	U	B	I	V	Z	T	H	M	O	T	M	R

1. Chores **2.** Dogwalk **3.** Babysitting **4.** Tutoring **5.** Lemonade **6.** Working

7. Helping **8.** Allowance **9.** Crafts **10.** Recycling **11.** Carwash **12.** Shoveling

13. Yardwork **14.** Errands **15.** Delivery **16.** Cleaning

Earnings

Different ways to earn

Instructions: Circle all the ways these kids are ***EARNING*** money.

Bonus Task: In the blank area, draw another way ***YOU*** can earn money.

Earnings

How many coins can you count

Earnings

True or False Earning Money Quiz

Instructions: Circle **True** if the statement is correct. Circle **False** if the statement is incorrect.

1. People once used shells as money. → **True or False**
2. Money once grew on trees. → **True or False**
3. The first paper money was invented in China. → **True or False**
4. The word "salary" comes from the word "salt," which was once used as money. → **True or False**
5. All coins in the world are made of gold. → **True or False**
6. Some countries have printed money made out of plastic instead of paper. → **True or False**
7. The U.S. once printed a $100,000 bill. → **True or False**
8. A piggy bank is called that because real pigs were once used to guard money. →**True or False**
9. In some parts of history, cocoa beans were used as money. → **True or False**
10. The smallest amount of money ever made was a half penny. → **True or False**
11. You can spend Monopoly money at a real store. → **True or False**
12. Coins have ridges (lines) on the edges to stop people from shaving off metal. → **True or False**
13. All countries use dollars as their money. → **True or False**
14. Some people earn money by playing video games professionally. → **True or False**
15. The $1 bill lasts about 6 months before it wears out. → **True or False**
16. Bitcoin is a type of digital money that doesn't exist in paper or coin form. → **True or False**
17. The first ATM machine was installed in the 1800s. → **True or False**
18. Before banks existed, people sometimes buried their money in the ground. → **True or False**
19. The U.S. penny used to be made mostly of copper. → **True or False**
20. There has never been a coin worth more than $1. → **True or False**

Earnings

How Long Will It Take

Jack really wants a new cell phone that costs $400.
He earns $40 each time he cuts a yard.
How many yards will Jack need to cut, to reach his goal?
About how long do you think it will take him?

Jack needs to cut _____ yards to reach his goal of $400.
How long will it take Jack to reach his goal of $400, if he cuts two yards per week? ________

Mia has her eyes on a cool new bike that costs $300.
She earns $25 each time she helps her neighbor do laundry and fold clothes.

How many times will Mia need to help with laundry to earn enough for her bike? __________
How long will it take Mia if she helps twice each week? __________

Liam wants to adopt a puppy that will cost $300, including supplies.
He earns $15 every time he walks a dog in his neighborhood.

How many dogs will Liam need to walk, to reach his goal of $300? ________
How long will it take Liam to reach his goal, if he walks four dogs every week? ________

Earnings

How Long Will It Take

Allan's Goal: Cool Headphones

Allan wants wireless **headphones** that cost $120.
He earns **$15** each time he washes his family's car.

Question 1: How many car washes will Allan need to do to pay for his headphones?

Answer: ___________

Question 2: If he washes **one car per week,** how long will it take?

Answer: ___________

Rachel's Goal: Tablet Upgrade

Rachel wants a **new tablet** that costs **$300**.
She earns **$30** each time she helps her aunt organize files and papers.

Question 1: How many times will Rachel need to help to earn her tablet?

Answer: ___________

Question 2: If she helps **twice a week**, how long will it take?

Answer: ___________

Ethan's Goal: New Sneakers

Ethan wants a pair of **sneakers** that cost **$150**.
He earns **$10** each time he takes out the trash for his neighbors.

Question 1: How many times will Ethan need to take out the trash to buy his sneakers?

Answer: ___________

Question 2: If he does this chore **three times per week**, how long will it take?

Answer: ___________

Earnings

Getting Your First Job

Work Forms: Getting Ready to Get Paid

W-4 Form — You fill this out when you start a job. It tells your employer how much tax to take out of your paycheck.

W-2 Form — You get this at the end of the year. It shows how much money you earned and how much tax you paid. You'll use it when filing your taxes.

Time Sheet / Time Card — Tracks how many hours you worked. Your boss uses it to calculate your pay.

Look at Isaiah, he worked hard for his first paycheck. But wait... what are all those numbers on his pay stub?

Let's break it down so he knows exactly where his money goes!

Deductions — Money taken out for taxes, Social Security, Medicare, or other benefits.

What is the total of Isaiah's current deductions?

$________________

Gross Pay — The total amount you earn ***before*** anything is taken out.

What is Isaiah's gross pay?

$________________

Net Pay — What's left ***after*** deductions, the amount you actually take home.

What is Isaiah's net pay?

$________________

ACME CORP

PAYSTUB

PAY PERIOD: 01/01/2024 - 01/14/2024

EMPLOYEE INFORMATION

Name: Johnson		**EARNINGS**
Isaiah Johnson	CURRENT	CURRENT
Address	80	YTD
123 Maple St, Anytown, USA	860	160
Regular Hours	Hourly Rate	$20.00
ID: 12345	$20.00	$20.00
GROSS PAY:		**$1600.00**

DEDUCTIONS

Description	Amount
Federal Tax	
State Tax	$160.00
Social Security	$80.20
Medicare	$23.20

TOTAL DECUCTIONS:

$263.40	**$778.60**
CURRENT	**YTD**

NET PAY: $1336.60

Earnings

Help Bessie and Robert read their paystub

Playground Education

1234 Wellington Hill Street
Mattapan MA
United States
02126

Bessie Roberson

Earnings Statement

Employee ID	Period ending	Pay date	Check #
1234	2025-01-09	2025-01-16	123

Income	Gross pay	Deductions	Amount	YTD
Regular	$4,230.77	Federal Tax	$1404	$0.00
		State Tax	$498	$0.00
		Social Security	$506	$0.00
		Medicare	$145	$0.00

YTD gross	YTD deductions	YTD net pay	Gross pay	Deductions	Net pay
$0.00	$0.00	$0.00	$4,230.77	$2,553.00	$1,677.77

Bessie

Current Gross Pay

$ ____________

Current Deductions

$ ____________

Net Pay (Take home)

$ ____________

Robert Rufus
BestEng@yahoo.com
123 Milton Ave
United States
Massachusetts

Boston Engineering
pugsley0000@yahoo.com
987 Blue Hill Ave
United States
Massachusetts

Employee Name	Employee ID/SSN	Pay Date	Paycheck No.
Robert Rufus	123-34-1-0987	7/24/2025	567

Pay Period	Employment Type	Date Hired	Salary Type
7/3/2025 - 7/17/2025	Employee		Salary

Pay Frequency	Currency	Hours	Current Additions		Current Deductions	
Bi-weekly	United States Dollar	80.00	—	—	Federal Tax	999
					State Tax	438
					Social Security	279
					Medicare	301

Current Earnings	YTD Gross	YTD Deductions	YTD Net Pay	Net Pay
3,691.15	51,676.06	28,238	23,438.06	1,674.15

Robert

Current Gross Pay

$ ____________

Current Deductions

$ ____________

Net Pay (Take home)

$ ____________

Earnings

Choosing the Right-After School Job

After-school jobs help you earn money for savings, spending, and future goals. However, not all jobs are created equal! When choosing a job, you have to consider pay, distance, and "hidden costs" like travel time or bus fare.

Instructions: Compare the job options below and help Ruby choose the one that best fits her goals.

Job Option	Hourly Wage	Commute Time (Round Trip)	Transportation Cost (Daily)
Job A (Retail Clerk)	$18.00	1.5 hours	$9.00 (Bus:$3.00, Train: $6.00)
Job B (Library Assistant)	$14.00	15 minutes	$0.00 (Walking)
Job C (Tutor)	$16.00	45 Minutes	$3.00 (One Bus)

Now You Decide

Which job pays the most per hour?

____

Which jobs cost money to travel to?

____

Which job(s) is closest to Ruby's home and school?

____

Which job do you think Ruby should take? Why?

____

Reflection Box

What is one thing ***you*** would consider most important if choosing a job?

____

Earnings

Now let's Help Gene Choose the Right After-School Job

Gene is saving up for a new gaming console and is exploring after-school job options. He needs to carefully weigh the **hourly pay** against the **time commitment** and **transportation costs** for each job.

Job Option	Hourly Wage	Commute Time (Round Trip)	Commute Cost (Round Trip)
Job A (Grocery Store Clerk)	$17.00	1 hour	**$6.00** (Two Bus Rides)
Job B (Dishwasher at Local Diner)	$15.50	20 minutes	**$0.00** (Biking)
Job C (Community Center Assistant)	$16.50	40 minutes	**$4.00** (One Bus)

Now You Decide

Which job pays the most per hour?

____

Which job(s) costs money to travel to?

____

Which job is closest to Gene's home and school?

____

Which job do you think Gene should take? Why?

____

Reflection Box

Considering the time and money spent on transportation, which job offers the highest **Net Hourly Wage** and leaves Gene with the most *free time* for schoolwork and activities?

____

Think about it: Is the $17.00/hour job worth it if it takes Gene an hour to commute every day and costs him $3.00 just to get there? Or is the $15.50/hour job better because Gene can bike and save that time and money? He is deciding between **higher gross pay** and **higher value of time**.

Earnings

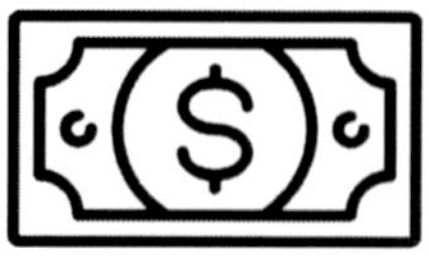

What Will I Be? Exploring Careers

Use these websites to explore different careers and learn about them.

https://www.careeronestop.org/
https://www.bls.gov/

Search for the career **nurse** on one of the websites listed

Find:

Job Description

____

____

____

Salary (Salary Range)

____

Skills / Education (Any other important details)

____

____

____

____

____

Earnings

Time to explore!

Instructions: Select two careers you are curious about and want to explore. Use the provided websites to research the daily responsibilities, the average salary, and the specific skills or education required for each role. Compare your findings in the space provided below.

https://www.careeronestop.org/

https://www.bls.gov/

Career 1: ______________________________

What the job does (Responsibilities): ______________________________

____

____

How much it pays (Salary): ______________________________

Skills or schooling needed: ______________________________

____

Career 2: ______________________________

What the job does (Responsibilities): ______________________________

____

____

How much it pays (Salary): ______________________________

Skills or schooling needed: ______________________________

____

Welcome to the Bank!

What a bank does => A safe place to keep, store, track, and transfer your money.

Banks have many ways to help you manage your money, including checking accounts and savings accounts.

Spending vs. Stashing: Checking accounts are for your **"now"** money, while savings accounts are for your **"later"** money.

Instructions: List *two* things you would pay for this week using a checking account. *Then,* List two big-picture goals you want to set aside money for in a savings account.

Type of Account	What It's Used For	Example
Checking Account	Spending money now (debit card, paying bills)	
Savings Account	Stashing money for later (for example: new laptop, car, or an emergency fund)	

Opening Your First Account (Under 18)

If you're under 18, follow these steps to get started:

- **The Partnership:** You must open a **joint account** with a parent or guardian. This means you both "own" the account, and you both sign the legal paperwork.
- **The ID Checklist:** You'll need to bring:
  - Full Names & Birthdates for both of you.
  - Social Security Numbers for both of you.
  - Valid Photo IDs (like a Driver's License, State ID, or Passport).
- **The "Buy-In":** You'll need a **first deposit**. While some banks require $25, many only require $5 or $10 to get started.

Massachusetts Pro-Tip (The 18/65 Law): To learn how this law protects you from bank fees, flip to the **"Key Resources"** section on **page 80** at the back of this book.

Earnings

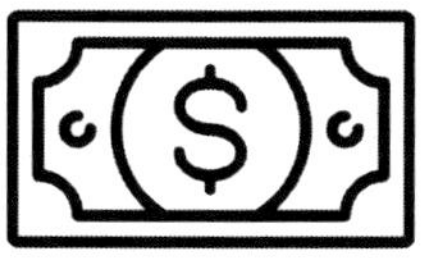

Build Your Banking Knowledge

Instructions: Match each banking vocabulary word to the correct definition.

Word Bank

Withdraw	Direct Deposit	Fee
Deposit	Debit Card	Overdraft
Balance	Interest	Statement
Credit Union	Mobile Banking	PIN

Banking Word	**Definition**
____________________	How much money you have right now.
____________________	A card that lets you spend your own money in your checking account.
____________________	The act of taking money *out* of your account.
____________________	Money the bank pays you for keeping your money there.
____________________	Putting money *into* your bank account.
____________________	Your paycheck goes straight into your bank account.
____________________	A member-owned, not-for-profit financial institution where members join together to save and borrow money. Unlike a bank, it is owned and operated by its members, not by outside investors or a corporation.
____________________	A secret number used to keep your debit card safe.
____________________	An amount of money a financial institution charges for a specific service or as a penalty for breaking an account rule (such as an overdraft fee or an out-of-network ATM charge).
____________________	When you spend more money than you have in your account.
____________________	A monthly record that shows how much money was spent and saved.
____________________	Using a smartphone or device to conduct financial transactions through a bank's app or website.

Earnings

Discover a Bank in Your Community

Instructions:
Use your ZIP code or city to search for banks (or credit unions) near you. Pick two banks (or credit unions), then fill in the information below to learn if either of these could be good places for your checking or savings account.

Name of the Bank (or Credit Union):

Bank's address (or how far it is from your home)

Do they offer Teen or Student Checking Accounts?

Do they offer a Savings Account?

What other services do they provide?
(ex. ATM card, mobile app, financial education, debit card)

Are There Any Fees?
(ex. Monthly fees, ATM fees, Overdraft fees)

Name of the Bank (or Credit Union):

Bank's address (or how far it is from your home)

Do they offer Teen or Student Checking Accounts?

Do they offer a Savings Account?

What other services do they provide?
(ex. ATM card, mobile app, financial education, debit card)

Are There Any Fees?
(ex. Monthly fees, ATM fees, Overdraft fees)

Earnings Reflection 

Instructions: Reflect on what you have learned in ***The Land of Earnings*** unit. Then answer the questions below.

Curious Questions

What am I still wondering about?

Money I Know

What ideas do I understand now?

My Next Money Move

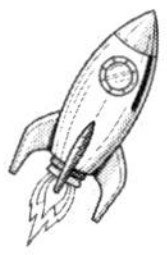

What will I do next?

What three ideas you're ready to take off with?

1.

2.

3.

Chapter 2: The Island of Savings

Instructions: Draw a line from the ***"Savings"*** word to its definition

Savings Word Match

Piggy Bank	Something you are saving money for, like a bike, a game, or a trip.
Interest	A plan for how you will spend and save your money.
Goal	Extra money you earn from the bank for keeping your savings there.
Deposit	A safe place (like a jar or little bank) where you put your money to save.
Budget	Putting money into a bank account or savings spot.

Savings Scramble

Instructions: Unscramble the ***"Savings"*** words you may know

SNOIC: ____________________

CUNTOAC: ____________________

EFAS: ____________________

GVISSNA: ____________________

AKNB: ____________________

Savings

Quiz: True or False

1. Saving means keeping money for later. (T/F)

2. You should spend 100% of your income every month to ensure your checking account balance is zero. (T/F)

3. A savings jar can help you reach your goals. (T/F)

Game: "Savings Race"

If you save $2 a week, how many weeks will it take to buy a $20 toy?

____

Activity: Fill the Jar

Your goal is to save **$20**! In the jar below, each dotted line represents a **$2 milestone**. Shade the jar upwards, level by level, until you reach your goal.

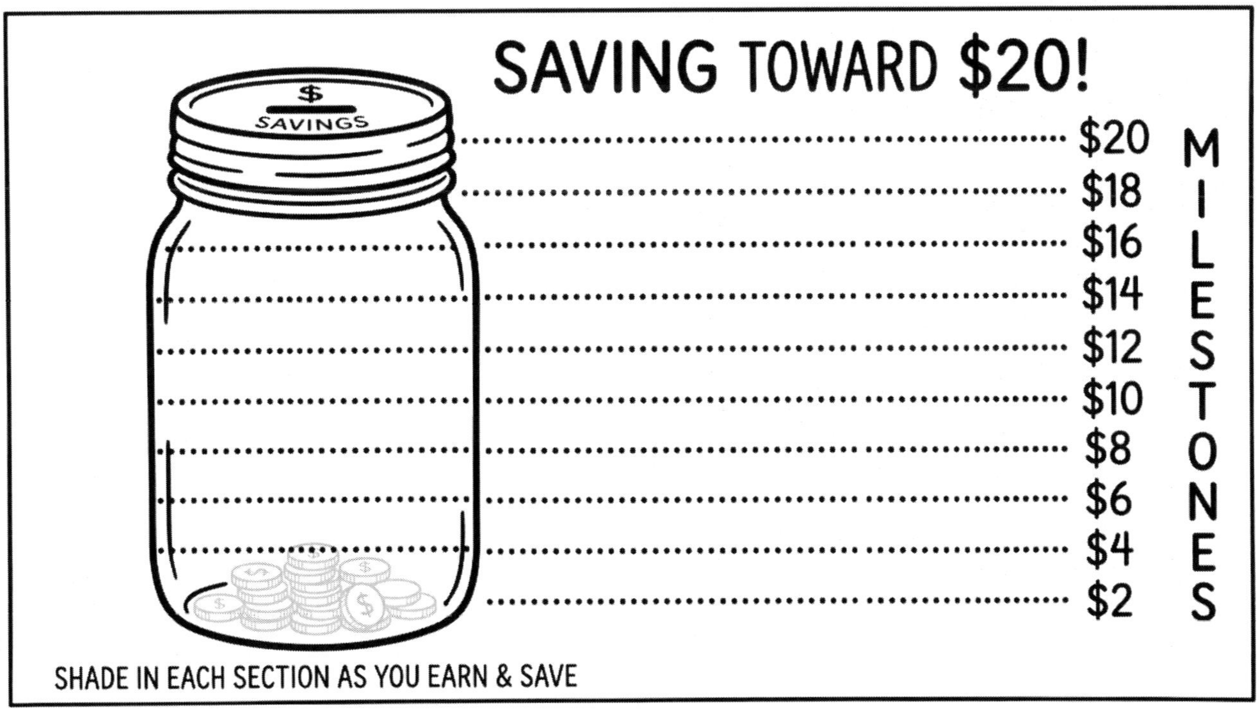

Savings

Savings Crossword

Savings

Across

5. The act of taking money *out* of your account
6. An unexpected situation when you might need to use your savings
10. Money given to you regularly, often for chores or good behavior
11. Something important that you must have, like food or shelter, which you might save for
12. To put money into a bank account
13. To keep a record of what you spend and save
15. A small container used to store spare coins and savings

Down

1. Using money to buy things you want or need
2. A plan that shows how much money you earn, spend, and save
3. To keep money instead of spending it right away
4. A step-by-step way to reach your savings goal
7. Something you're saving money for in the future
8. A safe place to keep your money and earn interest
9. Extra money the bank gives you for keeping your savings there
14. A record at a bank showing how much money you have saved

Can You Crack the Savings Code?

Instructions:
Each number stands for a letter. Use the decoding chart below to figure out the secret savings message. When you finish, read it out loud to learn one of the smartest money tips ever shared!

Decoder Key Table

A=1 B=2 C=3 D=4 E=5 F=6 G=7 H=8 I=9 J=10 K=11 L=12 M=13 N=14

O=15 P=16 Q=17 R=18 S=19 T=20 U=21 V=22 W=23 X=24 Y=25 Z=26

The Coded Message

4 15 14 15 20 19 1 22 5 23 8 1 20 9 19 12 5 6 20
1 6 20 5 18 19 16 5 14 4 9 14 7 ;
9 14 19 20 5 1 4 , 19 16 5 14 4 23 8 1 20 9 19 12 5 6 20
1 6 20 5 18 19 1 22 9 14 7 .

Decode the message here:

Quote attributed to Warren Buffett

Savings

PUGSLEY'S CODED RIDDLE

Change each letter to the one that comes immediately ***BEFORE*** it in the alphabet to find Pugsly's Riddle and its answer.

Here's a copy of the alphabet to guide you

a b c d e f g h i j k l m n o p q r s t u v w x y z

Riddle: J'n xifsf fwfsz epmmbs hpft, uibu't uif qmbo.

____

J tupq zpvs npofz gspn tmjqqjoh bxbz

____

boe ifmq zpvs tbwjoht hspx fbdi ebz.

____

Answer: Cvehfu

____

Savings

Learn from Nature's Savers

These amazing animals and insects know how to plan ahead

Instructions: Match each animal and insect to the way it saves or stores its food. Just like these clever creatures, you'll discover that saving helps you stay ready for your own future!

Squirrels ____

a Build lodges and store branches underwater for food during cold months

Beavers ____

b Drill holes in trees to store acorns

Ants ____

c Make and store honey in their hives for food when flowers aren't blooming

Woodpeckers ____

d Stuff food in their cheek pouches to carry and store in their burrows

Honey Bees ____

e Hide acorns and nuts in the ground to eat during winter

Hamsters ____

f Collect seeds and crumbs during summer to survive the winter

"Just like animals prepare for winter, we prepare for our future by saving money!"

Savings Reflection

Instructions: Reflect on what you have learned in ***The Island of Saving*** unit. Then answer the questions below.

Curious Questions

What am I still wondering about?

Money I Know

What ideas do I understand now?

My Next Money Moves

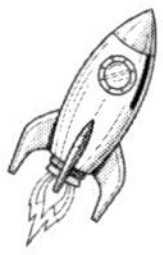

What will I do next?

What three ideas you're ready to take off with?

1.

2.

3.

Chapter 3: The Town of Spending

GAME: Needs vs Wants

Instructions: Look at each item below. Circle the word that describes it: is it a ***NEED*** or a ***WANT*** ?

Want or Need

Want or Need

Want or Need

Want or Need

Want or Need

Want or Need

Want or Need

Want or Need

School Supplies

Want or Need

Designer shoes $300

Want or Need

Spending

Game: $10 Dollar X 2 Challenge

Scenario: You've earned $10. In the table below, write down two ideas for how you would Spend, Save, and Share your new income.

Spend:

____

____

Save:

____

____

Share or Give:

____

____

Spending

Smart Shopping

Store A

Store B

Vanessa's Headphones

Vanessa wants a pair of wireless headphones that cost **$80**.

- Store A: **$20 off** the price.
- Store B: **30% off** the price.

☞ Which deal should Vanessa choose?

Answer: ___________

Noah's Sneakers

Noah found sneakers that cost **$120**.

- Store A: **$15 off**
- Store B: **20% off**

☞ Which deal gives Noah the better price?

Answer: ___________

Spending

Smart Shopping

Store A

Store B

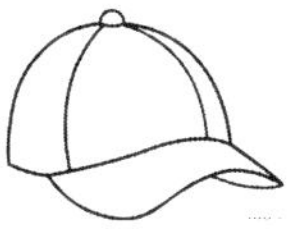

Reggie's New Hat

Reggie wants a stylish hat that normally costs **$40**

- Store A: **$10 off** the price.
- Store B: **25% off** the price.

☞ Which deal should Reggie choose?

Answer: ___________

Jasmine's Video Game

Jasmine wants a new video game that costs **$60**.

- Store A: **$10 off**
- Store B: **15% off**

☞ Which deal gives Jasmine the better price?

Answer: ___________

Spending

The Budget Game – Life in a Month

Objective: Learn how to make a budget, track expenses, and adjust for unexpected costs, while keeping your finances balanced!

How to Play:

You have a **monthly income of $200** (allowance, chores, birthday money, etc.). You must decide how to spend, save, and manage your money for the month. The goal is to **end the month with at least $20 left over**.

Step 1: Plan Your Budget

Use this chart to plan your spending before the month begins.

Category	**Suggested %**	**My Budget ($)**
Savings	20%	______
Food & Snacks	15%	______
Entertainment	15%	______
Clothing & Shopping	15%	______
Gifts & Giving	10%	______
School & Supplies	15%	______
Other / Extra	10%	______
Total	**100%**	**$200**

Tip: A good budget always adds up to your total income.

Spending

The Budget Game – Life in a Month

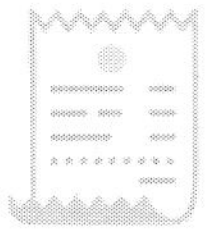

Step 2: Life Happens!

Each student rolls "Money Dice" or picks random "Life Cards" (you can print these in your workbook to draw or flip).
Each card changes a student's budget. Some for better, some for worse.

Budget Game "Life Cards"

Card	Event	Effect
Birthday money!	You get $25 extra!	+$25
Impulse buy	You spent $15 on a game you didn't plan for.	-$15
Gift for a friend	You bought a birthday present for $10.	-$10
Lost your bus pass	Replaced it for $5.	-$5
Extra chores	You earned $20!	+$20
Pizza party	You spent $8 with friends.	-$8
Smart spender bonus	You compared prices and saved $10!	+$10
Cracked your phone case	New one cost $12.	-$12

Students pick **3–4 cards** and adjust their budgets accordingly.

Budget Game: Life Cards

Spending

■ Birthday Money! Grandma sent you a surprise envelope. **+ $25**	**■ Extra Chores** You helped wash cars on the weekend. **+ $20**	**■ Smart Spender** You used a coupon and saved money. **+ $10**
■ Book Sale Win Found your schoolbook used for cheap! **+ $8**	**■ Scholarship Gift** Good grades earned you a reward. **+ $15**	**■ Sold Old Game** You sold a used game online. **+ $18**
■ Allowance Raise Parents gave you a small raise! **+ $10**	**■ Clean Room Bonus** You got $5 for keeping things spotless. **+ $5**	**■ Pet-Sitting Job** Earned cash walking your neighbor's dog. **+ $12**
■ Creative Hustle Sold handmade bracelets at school. **+ $10**	**■ Goal Bonus** You reached a savings milestone. **+ $10**	**■■ Rainy-Day Saver** You skipped spending this week! **+ $15**
■ Pizza Party Fun night out with friends. **- $8**	**■ Impulse Buy** Bought something not in your plan. **- $15**	**■ Gift for a Friend** You bought a thoughtful birthday gift. **- $10**
■ Cracked Phone Case Had to replace it fast. **- $12**	**■ Lost Bus Pass** Bought a new one right away. **- $5**	**■ Snack Attack** Daily snacks add up quickly. **- $7**

Budget Game: Life Cards

Spending

■ New Trend Splurged on that cool hoodie. **- $25**	**■ Sports Fee** Paid to join your favorite team. **- $20**	**■ Toy Temptation** Couldn't resist that plush toy. **- $9**
■ Tablet Trouble Needed a new charger. **- $10**	**■ Online Shopping** Bought something on sale… again. **- $14**	**■ Forgotten Bill** You had to pay your club dues. **- $6**
■ Vet Visit Pet got sick — learned responsibility! **- $10**	**■ Field Trip Fun** School adventure - worth the price. **- $20**	**■ Borrowed Money** Borrowed from a friend, pay back soon. **- $10**
■ Smart Saver Waited a week and found a deal! **+ $5**	**■■ Limited-Time Sale** Saved $10 on something planned. **+ $10**	**■ Goal Check** Reached your savings goal, small reward! **- $5**
■■ Shopping Trade-Off Bought sneakers, skipped a T-shirt. **Even**	**■ Budget Review** Overspent by $10 last week — lesson learned. **- $10**	**■ Found Money** Found $2 in your jeans pocket! **+ $2**
■ Helping Hand Donated $5 to a good cause. **- $5**	**■ Mini Business** Sold plants from your garden. **+ $8**	**■ Forgot to Plan** Missed a sale and overpaid $10. **- $10**

Spending

Step 3: Adjust and Reflect

Category	Planned ($) From Step 1	Actual($)	Difference
Savings	______	______	______
Food	______	______	______
Entertainment	______	______	______
Shopping	______	______	______
Gifts and Giving	______	______	______
School	______	______	______
Other	______	______	______
Total Spent	______	______	______
Money Left/Short	______		

Did you stay within your budget? If not, what caused you to overspend?

____

____

What would you change next month to do better?

____

____

Spending

Reflection Zone

1. What did you learn about planning before spending?

____

____

2. Which "Life Card" surprised you the most?

____

____

3. How did your savings help your final budget?

____

____

Spending

Key Takeaway

Budgeting helps you control your money ***before it controls you!***
The better you plan, the more freedom you have to spend, save, and smile later.

Bonus Activity: My Smart Savings Goal

I'm saving for: ______________________________

Total Goal: $___________

Saved So Far: $___________

Goal Date: ___________________________

One thing I'll do to reach my goal faster:

____

____

____

Spending

Slice of My Budget Pie!

Theme Concept:
Imagine you just received a set amount of money (realistic allowance or part-time earnings). You have to decide how to divide your ***"money pie"*** into slices for ***saving, spending, sharing,*** **and** ***surprises.***

Jasmine earned **$100** this month! 
Her job is to decide how to *slice her budget pie.*
How much will she spend? How much will she save? Will she give any away?
She fills in the chart below.

Jasmine's Budget Chart Table

Category	*Description*	*Amount*	* *% of Total*
Savings	Money you keep for goals or emergencies	$25	25%
Spending	Things you buy now (snacks, games, outings)	$45	45%
Sharing	Gifts or donations to others	$10	10%
Surprises	Unexpected costs or fun treats	$20	20%
Total		**$100**	**100%**

* Find your % by doing: (Your amount ÷ 100) × 100 = Your percent!

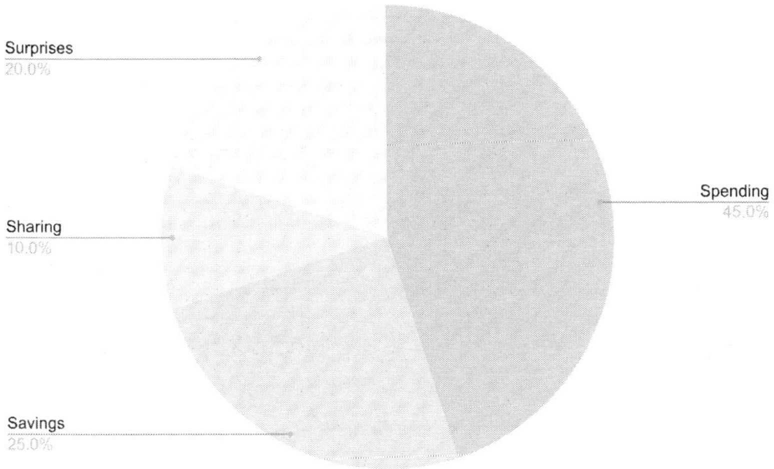

Which slice of Jasmine's pie is the biggest? Why?

____

If Jasmine needed to grow her "Savings" slice, what could she cut down on?

____

What would happen if Jasmine's "Spending" slice kept getting bigger?

____

____

*Discussion question: Why do you think "**Savings**" is listed first?*

Your Turn

Spending

Slice of Your Budget Pie!

You earned **$150** this month!
Decide how to slice your budget pie.
How much will you spend? How much will you save? Will you give any away?
Fill in the chart below.

Your Budget Chart Table

Category	Description	Amount	* % of Total
Savings	Money you keep for goals or emergencies	$	%
Spending	Things you buy now (snacks, games, outings)	$	%
Sharing	Gifts or donations to others	$	%
Surprises	Unexpected costs or fun treats	$	%
Total		**$150**	**100%**

* Find your % by doing: (Your amount ÷ 100) × 100 = Your percent!

Divide your pie chart into slices that match your percentages. Label each slice with its category name and percent.

Which slice of your pie is the biggest? Why?

If your pie needed to grow a bigger "Savings" slice, what could you cut down on?

What would happen if your "Spending" slice kept getting bigger?

Spending

"Where Did the Money Go?" — Jasmine's Budgeting Story

Help Jasmine complete her budgeting story!

Instructions: Use the words from the word bank to fill in each blank. Choose the word that fits best in the sentence.

Allocation	Assets	Budget (used twice)	Cash Flow
Cost of Living	Deductions	Discretionary Spending	Disposable Income
Emergency Fund	Expenses	Fixed Expenses	Gross Pay
Income	Liabilities	Needs	Net Pay
Savings	Variable Expenses	Wants	

Jasmine had just graduated and landed a great part-time job as a social media coordinator, dreaming of eventually opening her own chic café. Her first major adult task was crafting a realistic ______________________________. She knew managing her money was the foundation of her future café empire.

Jasmine's job paid her $20 an hour. Before taxes and other withholdings, her paycheck amounted to $1,600 for the month, this was her __________________________. However, once the government took out ______________________________ for taxes and retirement savings, the actual amount deposited into her bank account was $1,300. This take-home amount was her crucial __________________________. She also had a small side hustle tutoring, which brought her a reliable $200 monthly. This entire stream of money coming in was her ______________________________.

Next, Jasmine listed everything she had to pay for. Her rent of $500 for a shared apartment and her student loan payment of $150 were the same every month, these were her ______________________________.

Then came the things that changed. Groceries, electricity, and gas for her scooter can fluctuate based on her usage. She categorized these as ______________________.

Spending

These necessary payments for survival, like rent and food, were her basic ____________________.

The remaining money after her fixed costs and essentials was her ___________________________.
She decided how much of this money should go to different categories, a process called
____________________________.

Jasmine loved a good weekend outing, which included brunch and, yes, the occasional expensive slice of gourmet avocado toast. The money she spent on movies, clothes, and those weekend treats was her ____________________________________ items that were not essential, but nice to have, or her ____________________________________.

In total, her monthly payments for everything, rent, food, loans, and fun, amounted to her total ____________________________________. She noticed that the local ______________________________________ was high, making it a challenge to cover all her expenses comfortably.

Jasmine was determined to be financially secure. She regularly put $250 a month into an ______________________________________, a special savings account meant only for unexpected life events, like a scooter repair or a medical bill. An additional $100 went into her long-term ____________________________________ for her café dream.

She knew a true financial picture required looking at her ___________________________ (like the value of her scooter and her savings accounts) and her _____________________ (her student loan debt).

At the end of the month, she reviewed her account. Did the money flowing in (Income) exceed the money flowing out (Expenses)? If so, she had a positive ___________________________________ .
Her goal was to always have a positive cash flow so she could keep building her future.

Jasmine realized her well-thought-out ____________________________________ wasn't just a list of numbers; it was the blueprint for her Avocado Toast Empire.

Spending

Paws and Payments:
Planning for a Pet - Can I Afford a Pet?

Step 1 Choose Your Pet: ______________________________

Step 2 Calculate the cost of owning your pet

Cost Category	What I Found (Price)	How often? (one-time/ monthly/yearly)	My Notes
Adoption Fee	$ ________	________	______________
Food	$ ________	________	______________
Toys / Bed / Bowl	$ ________	________	______________
Vet Check-Ups	$ ________	________	______________
Flea / Tick / Heartworm	$ ________	________	______________
Grooming (if needed)	$ ________	________	______________
Emergency Fund	$ ________	________	______________

Step 3 Total Monthly Pet Cost **$**________

Step 4 My Budget Check

My Monthly Discretionary Income $ ________ Total Monthly Pet Cost $ ________

Can I afford it?

☐ **Yes** ☐ **No**

Her are some websites to research pet adoption costs

Petfinder	https://www.petfinder.com
Adopt-a-Pet	https://www.adoptapet.com
ASPCA	https://www.aspca.org/pet-care

Spending

Technology Upgrade vs. Old Technology

Clover has **$1,200** in her savings account and urgently needs a functional laptop for school. She is trying to decide how to spend her money. She has three choices. Help her analyze the total cost and value of each option.

Option A: The Newest Model (High Cost): A brand new laptop for $1,200. It will last for many years and has the best features, but it drains all of Clover's savings.

Option B: A Refurbished/Older Model (Medium Cost): A slightly older or professionally refurbished model for $600. It works well for school and gaming but Clover may need to replace this one sooner.

Option C: Repairing the Current Model (Low Cost): Spending $150 to fix the screen on her existing device, allowing Clover to keep the rest of her savings.

Part 1: Help Clover analyze the total cost and value of each option.

Option	**Description**	**Price**	**Estimated Lifespan**	**Annual Cost (Price ÷ Lifespan)**
A: Newest Model	Brand-new, high-end laptop with all the features.	$1,200	5 years	________
B: Refurbished Model	A reliable, certified pre-owned model.	$600	3 years	________
C: Repair	Repair her current broken laptop screen.	$150	1 year (expected)	________

Reflection: Based **solely** on the Annual Cost, which option is the most financially efficient?

Answer: ________________

Spending

Continue helping Clover

Part 2: Trade-Off Scenario Questions

Instructions: Answer the following questions using complete sentences.

1. If Clover chooses **Option A ($1,200)**, how much money will she have left in her savings? $ ______________
   - *Question:* What is the risk of spending all of her savings on a new laptop? ____

     ____
2. If Clover chooses **Option C ($150)**, she keeps most of her savings.
   - *Question:* What is the non-financial risk (related to performance or reliability) of choosing to repair her old laptop instead of buying a new one?

     ____

     ____

Decision: If you were Clover, and you knew you had another year of school after this one, which option would you choose and why?__________________

____

Part 3: Research and Fill-in-the-Blank

Instructions: Use the internet to research and fill in the blanks with the correct financial terms.

- The rapid decrease in the value of a new technology item over time is called ______________________.
- When you choose one option (like buying a new laptop) over another (like keeping your savings), the value of the next best option you gave up is called the ______________________________ cost.
- A ______________________________ purchase refers to buying a slightly older, professionally reconditioned electronic item, which often saves money.

Spending

The End-of-Year Trip Decision: France vs. Spain

Randi has saved $2,700 and must decide between the two end-of-year trips, but she has learned that the **sticker price** is not the **true cost**, forcing her to analyze the total expenses for each destination.

Part 1: Trip Cost Comparison

Instructions: Help Randi compare the packages to find the true out-of-pocket costs and hidden fees.

Cost Category	Trip to France (French Club)	Trip to Spain (Spanish Class)
Package Price (Includes Airfare)	$2,200	$1,800
What's Included in Package?	Airfare, **ALL 6 nights hotel**, **ALL** local transport (bus/metro pass), daily breakfast.	Airfare, **2 nights hotel**, NO local transport, daily breakfast.
Nights Hotel	**$0** (All 6 nights covered)	____________ ($150/night **x 4 nights**)
Local Transportation	**$0** (Pass included)	____________ ($25/day **x 7 days**)
Required Tip/Insurance Fee	$100	$75
Meals (Lunches & Dinners)	____________ (Estimated $50/day **x 7 days**)	____________ (Estimated $45/day **x 7 days**)
Total Out-of-Pocket Costs	**A. $** ____________	**B. $** ____________

Spending

Part 2: Mathematical Analysis

Instructions: Calculate the final costs and determine which trip is actually the most affordable. (Randi still has **$2,700** saved).

1. Calculate Total Trip Cost (Trip A):
   $2,200 + Total Out-of-Pocket Costs (A) = 1.______________________
2. Calculate Total Trip Cost (Trip B):
   $1,800 + Total Out-of-Pocket Costs (B) = 2. ______________________
3. Final Comparison: Based on the Total Trip Cost, which destination is the better financial deal for Randi?
   Answer: ______________________

Part 3: Final Reflection

Instructions: Answer the following question based on your analysis of the trip costs.

Why is it important to look at the ***Total Cost*** of a trip (including all out-of-pocket expenses) rather than just the initial Package Price? Explain your answer using the example of the France vs. Spain trip comparison.

____

____

____

Spending

My First Vehicle: A Major Financial Decision

Buying a car is one of the largest financial commitments you'll make. It involves more than just the purchase price; it involves a **Total Cost of Ownership (TCO).** You need to budget for the recurring expenses that come with owning a car.

Help Jack analyze the **Total Cost of Ownership**: debt, interest, and recurring expenses (insurance & gas).

The Trade-Off: New vs. Used

Jack saved **$4,000** for a down payment and needs a reliable car for work and school. He has two options:

Option	Description	Purchase Price	Down Payment
Option A: New Sedan	Reliable, latest safety features, 5-year loan, **5% interest.**	$22,000	$4,000
Option B: Used Compact	3 years old, proven reliability, 3-year loan, **7% interest.**	$12,000	$4,000

Mathematical Analysis

Instructions: Calculate the total amount Jack needs to borrow (the Loan Amount) for each car.

1. **Option A Loan Amount:** Purchase Price - Down Payment = $22,000 - $4,000 =

   1. $ ________________

2. **Option B Loan Amount:** Purchase Price - Down Payment = $12,000 - $4,000 =

   2. $ ________________

Spending

Total Cost of Ownership (TCO) Calculation

The total cost of the car goes well beyond the purchase price. Use the monthly estimates below to calculate the total.

	Option A	Option B
Loan Payment	18,000 loan for 5 years at 5% will be about $339.63 monthly payments	8,000 loan for 3 years at 7% will be about $247.01 monthly payments
Insurance Premium	$220	$180
Fuel (Gas)	$150	$100
Maintenance/Repairs	$50 (Newer car, less required)	**$120.00** (Older car, more required)
Subtotal Monthly Payment	3. $ ____________	4. $ ____________

Total Annual Expense

Instructions: Calculate the total cost to own and operate each car for the entire first year.

3. **Option A Monthly Cost:** Sum of all monthly costs = 3. $ __________________
4. **Option B Monthly Cost:** Sum of all monthly costs = 4. $ __________________
5. **Option A Total Annual TCO:** Monthly Cost x 12 months = 5. $ __________________
6. **Option B Total Annual TCO:** Monthly Cost x 12 months = 6. $ __________________

Reflection, Decision, and Discussion Questions

Instructions: Use the financial results and common knowledge to answer the following questions.

1. TCO Analysis: Which car has a lower Total Cost of Ownership (TCO) in the first year? Answer: Option ________________
2. **Debt and Interest:** Which car carries a higher total cost due to **interest**? Why is the interest rate often higher on a used car loan (Option B) compared to a new car loan (Option A)?
3. **Depreciation:** What is **depreciation**? Why does buying a used car usually mean you suffer less from the effects of depreciation than buying a new car?
4. **Final Decision:** If Jack's monthly budget for transportation can't exceed $500, which car is the only responsible choice? Explain your reasoning using the calculated **Subtotal Monthly Payment**.

Spending Reflection

Instructions: Reflect on what you have learned in ***The Town of Spending*** unit. Then answer the questions below.

Curious Questions

What am I still wondering about?

Money I Know

What ideas do I understand now?

My Next Money Moves

What will I do next?

What three ideas you're ready to take off with?

1.

2.

3.

Chapter 4: The Garden of Growing Wealth

Growing Wealth - Fill In The Blanks

Assets	Compound	Profit
Bank (Savings)	Dividend	Risk
Budget	Income	Stock
Business	Invest	Value

A place where money grows with interest ____________________

Owning part of a company ________________________

Creating something to sell _______________________

To put money into something (like a business or stock) hoping it will grow in value

____

The money you make after paying for costs (expenses) _________________________

Things you own that have value, like a bike, computer, or even a house _____________

Money you receive from working, selling, or investing ______________________

The chance that you could lose money when investing _____________________

How much something is worth in money ____________________________

When interest is added to savings and starts earning more interest too ______________

A payment some companies give you if you own their stock _____________________

A plan that shows how much money you will spend and how much you will save ___________

Growing Wealth

Game: The Wealth Garden Challenge

Instructions: Grow your own garden of wealth by matching money concepts with the correct plants.

Below is your Wealth Garden! It has 6 empty spots waiting for plants. Each plant represents a money concept. As you play, fill each spot with the correct plant by matching the scenarios to the right financial term.

If you fill all 6 plant spots correctly, your garden is "thriving!"

(1) You spent all your money on video games and have nothing left to invest. (Which plant does this belong to?)

(2) You put $20 into a savings account and earn extra money over time. (Which plant does this belong to?)

(3) You sell lemonade for $5 after spending $2 on supplies. What's left is your____. (Which plant does this belong to?)

(4) You buy something (like stock or a business) hoping its value will grow. (Which plant does this belong to?)

(5) You own part of a company and it pays you a little money for being a shareholder. (Which plant does this belong to?)

(6) Your savings earn interest, and then that interest also earns interest. (Which plant does this belong to?)

PLANTS		
Savings Plant	Profit Tree	Investment Vine
Dividend Flower	Risk Weed	Compound Interest Tree

__________________ (1)

__________________ (2)

__________________ (3)

__________________ (5)

__________________ (4)

__________________ (6)

If you match all 6, your garden is ***"Thriving"***

Growing Wealth

Seed or Weed? Smart Spending Decisions

Instructions: Identify smart vs. wasteful financial choices.

Theme Concept:
Every financial decision is like planting a ***seed*** (it grows your wealth) or letting a ***weed*** (it drains your money) take over your garden.

Scenarios: Circle One

You pack lunch instead of buying fast food. Seed / Weed

Why? ______________________________

You buy a new video game before saving for your goal. Seed / Weed

Why? ______________________________

You start saving birthday money for a bike. Seed / Weed

Why? ______________________________

You buy snacks every day after school. Seed / Weed

Why? ______________________________

You do chores to earn extra money. Seed / Weed

Why? ______________________________

"What are three *money seeds* you can plant this week to help your wealth grow?"

1. ______________________________

2. ______________________________

3. ______________________________

Growing Wealth

Theme Concept: "Snakes in the Garden"

Just like real gardens have pests and snakes that can damage healthy plants, your ***wealth garden*** can be threatened by habits, choices, or traps that slow your financial growth. **Smart gardeners** (savvy money managers!) learn to spot and stop the snakes early.

Spot the Snake!

Instructions: Recognize ***financial traps*** like impulse buying, peer pressure, and scams.

Scenario Snake or Safe?	Circle One	**If you circled the snake, How would a Savvy Money Manager redirect their path?**
You spend all your allowance on snacks instead of saving.	✓	______________
Your friend tells you to buy matching shoes even though you don't have enough money	✓	______________
You compare prices before buying and save $30.	✓	______________
You get tricked by an online ad and lose $50.	✓	______________
You write down your savings goal and stick to your plan.	✓	______________
You borrow $20 from a friend and forget to pay them back.	✓	______________
You wait a week before buying something to see if you still want it.	✓	______________

"Which snake has tried to sneak into *your* financial garden before? How will you keep it out next time?"

____

____

Growing Wealth

My Weekly Garden Growth Log

Theme Concept:
"Water" your money garden by saving or making wise spending decisions. Each week record one action that helped your wealth "***grow***" and one ***"weed"*** you'll pull next week.

My Weekly Garden Growth Log

Week	What did I do to help my money grow	Did I spend or save this week	What will I do differently next week?
1	____________________ ____________________	Spent / Saved 	____________________ ____________________
2	____________________ ____________________	Spent / Saved 	____________________ ____________________
3	____________________ ____________________	Spent / Saved 	____________________ ____________________
4	____________________ ____________________	Spent / Saved 	____________________ ____________________

Looking back on your garden: What habit helped your wealth grow the most this month?

____

What's one "weed' (bad habit) you'll pull next month?

____

Growing Wealth

How to Grow Your Wealth from an Idea!
Planting Your Own Business

Little Kayla wants to be a "kidpreneur", which is a child or young person who starts their own business, creating products or offering services to the community.

While you help Kayla start her cupcake business, you can start your own business and you too can be a ***"Kidpreneur"***

Step 1: Dream It! (Plant Your Idea)

Every business starts with a seed, an idea

Kayla's Information

Kayla's idea: Selling Cupcakes

Help Kayla with a name for her business. Kayla is thinking about ***Kayla's Kupcakes***. Can you think of a another business name for Kayla?

____

____

Your Information

Your idea? ____________________

____

Brainstorm a name for your business name?

____

____

Step 2: Elevator Pitch (The Fast Seed) You've found the perfect seed for your business—your idea! Explain it in no more than two sentences. Tell us how much "sun" (hard work) and "water" (money) it needs to start growing fast.

Kayla's Kupcakes delivers allergy-friendly, custom cupcakes, the safe and magical solution for children's parties.We've proven our model, successfully catering 500+ events last year, but limited capacity is now costing us orders. We need $__ to secure a dedicated kitchen and vans, which will triple our production and allow us to immediately scale into three new markets. (Optional) We project investors will see a __% return in the third year.

Your Pitch: ____________________

____

____

(use another page if necessary)

Growing Wealth

Step 3: Make It Shine! (Stand Out in the Garden)

Every garden has lots of flowers, but what makes *yours* stand out?

Think about what makes your business **special and different** from others. Is it your **flavors**, your **name**, your **prices**, your **creative designs**, your **awesome logo**, or maybe your **great customer service**?

Your **"special touch"** is what helps your business bloom brighter than the rest!

Kayla's Special Touch

Business Name:
Kayla's Kupcakes

Can you think of any other great ideas to help Kayla's business stand out?

____

____

____

____

Your Special Touch

Brainstorm a few ways to make your business stand out.

____

____

____

____

____

____

Growing Wealth

Step 4: Plan It! (Water Your Garden)

Now, plan what you'll need to make your business grow!

Help Kayla with **research** for the cost of items

Kayla's Mini Budget Table

Item	What You Need	($)Cost
Ingredients	Flour, sugar, frosting, etc.	
Supplies	Baking pans, boxes, napkins	
Marketing	Posters, flyers, social media	
Helpers	Friends, family, classmates	
Start-Up Cost	Table, Pitcher, etc.	

Total Cost $ ____________

Can you think of any other items or materials Kayla needs to start her cupcake business?

____

____

Your Turn

Growing Wealth

Plan what you'll need to make your business grow!

Conduct a mini market research session: Look up the current prices for the top items you need to launch your business. Be sure to record the exact costs so your budget is as accurate as possible.

Your Mini Budget Table

Item	What (or how much) You Need	Cost ($)

Total Cost $ ____________

Use this space to list any other supplies or tools you'll need for your business. Can you borrow something, or find it cheap or free? Some things, like equipment, are one-time buys you can use again and again!

____

____

____

Growing Wealth

Step 5: Price It! (Let It Bloom!)

Help Kayla decide how much to charge and how much she'll earn!

Cupcake Price		Number Sold		Total Income	Profit (Income-Costs)
$ ________	X	______	=	$ ________	$ ____________

What ideas do you have for Kayla to increase her profits?

____

____

Your Information

Item Price or cost per service		Number Sold or number of services		Total Income	Profit (Income-Costs)
$ ________	X	______	=	$ ________	$ ____________

What ideas do you have to increase your profits?

____

____

Growing Wealth

Step 6: Reflect & Grow

Thinking Bigger: Helping My Business Grow

You've planted your business, watched it grow, and learned how to care for it!

Now it's time to think about what comes next.

Every great entrepreneur keeps dreaming, planning, and finding new ways to make their business bloom even bigger!

1. Expansion (Growing Bigger)

What could you do (or add) to your business to make it even better?

____

____

2. Avoiding Failure (Keeping It Strong)

Think about what could go wrong, and how to fix it before it happens.

____

____

3. Premium Offers (Something Special)

Some customers love extra-special touches, like fancy packaging or extra sprinkles. What **'premium' service** or **'special' product** could you offer?

____

4. Partnerships (Teamwork Makes it Grow)

Who could you work with to make your business stronger?

____

Growing Wealth Reflection

Instructions: Reflect on what you have learned in ***The Garden of Growing Wealth*** unit. Then answer the questions below.

Curious Questions

What am I still wondering about?

Money I Know

What ideas do I understand now?

My Next Money Moves

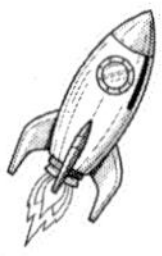

What will I do next?

What three ideas you're ready to take off with?

1.

2.

3.

Chapter 5: The Grove of Giving

Activity: My Giving Plan Journal Page

Write and draw your own plan for giving

Writing Section:

1. How I can give my time (Example: Volunteering): ____________________
2. How I can use my money to make a difference: ______________________
3. How I can use my talents to help others: _________________________

Activity: Grow Your Giving Tree

What kind of fruit will your tree grow? Below is your "Giving Tree." Draw the following symbols on the branches to show how you plan to help others:

Fruit = Giving Time or Talent

- Fruit grows when you care for a tree, just like giving grows when you share your time or talents.

Coins = Giving Treasure (Money or Resources)

- Coins represent money or material resources kids might give, even in small amounts.

Hearts = Giving Kindness or Care

- Hearts represent emotional giving, showing love, compassion, and kindness.

Giving

Activity: The Giving Grove Maze

Instructions: Guide the **coin character** through the maze to reach the **Giving Grove** at the end. Along the way, you'll make choices about ***how to use money and resources***.

The correct path is marked with **good giving choices**, while the wrong paths lead to **selfish or wasteful decisions**.

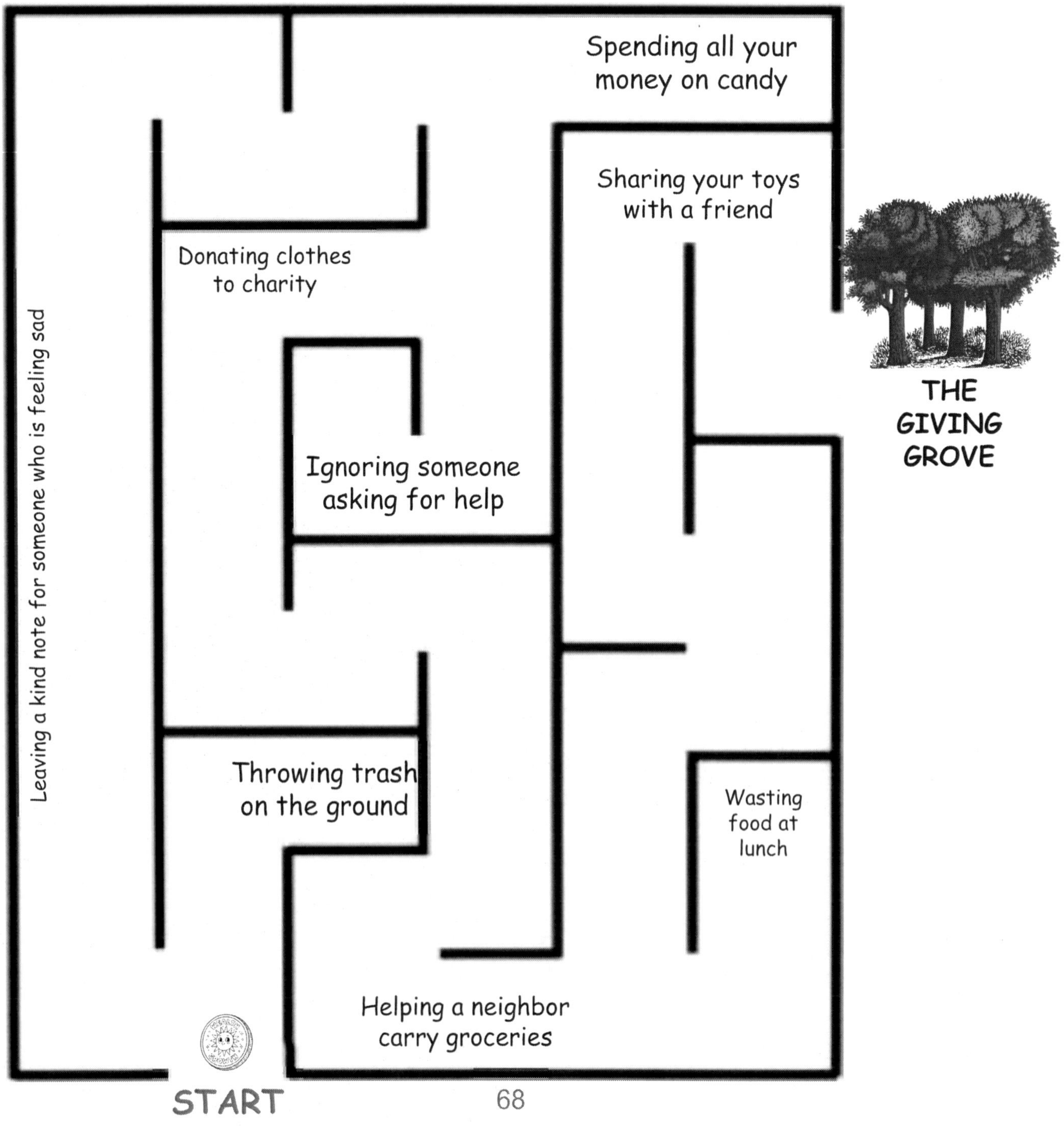

Giving

Pugsley's Giving Scrambler

Instructions: Unscramble the words in each clue to reveal words about **giving** and **kindness**. After you solve all the clues, find the **bold letters** in each answer and use them to complete **"Pugsley's Giving Phrase of the Day"** on the next page!

ndkine**s**s	Acting with care, compassion, and warmth
ht**a**ryic	Helping those in need through donations or service
v**r**es**i**ce	Helpful action performed for others
roe**ng**isyte	The quality of being kind and giving freely
nod**i**aton	Something, often money or goods, given to help others
nraghi**s**	Dividing and giving a portion to others
tronubti**c**oin	Something given to help achieve a goal or support others
aphtemy	Understanding and sharing another person's feelings
t**r**ulasim	The belief in or practice of selfless concern for others
compss**i**ano	Deep awareness of others' suffering with a desire to help
thylpharop**n**i	Promoting others' welfare through generous giving
fti**g**	Something voluntarily given without expecting payment

Giving

Pugsley's Giving Phrase Of The Day

____ ____ ____ ____ ____ ____ ____

____ ____   ____ ____ ____ ____ ____ ____

Giving

The Giving Tree Challenge

Theme: Acts of Kindness Grow Like Leaves

Instructions:

1. Look at the tree outline below (or draw your own!).
2. Whenever you perform or plan an act of kindness, record it on a leaf.

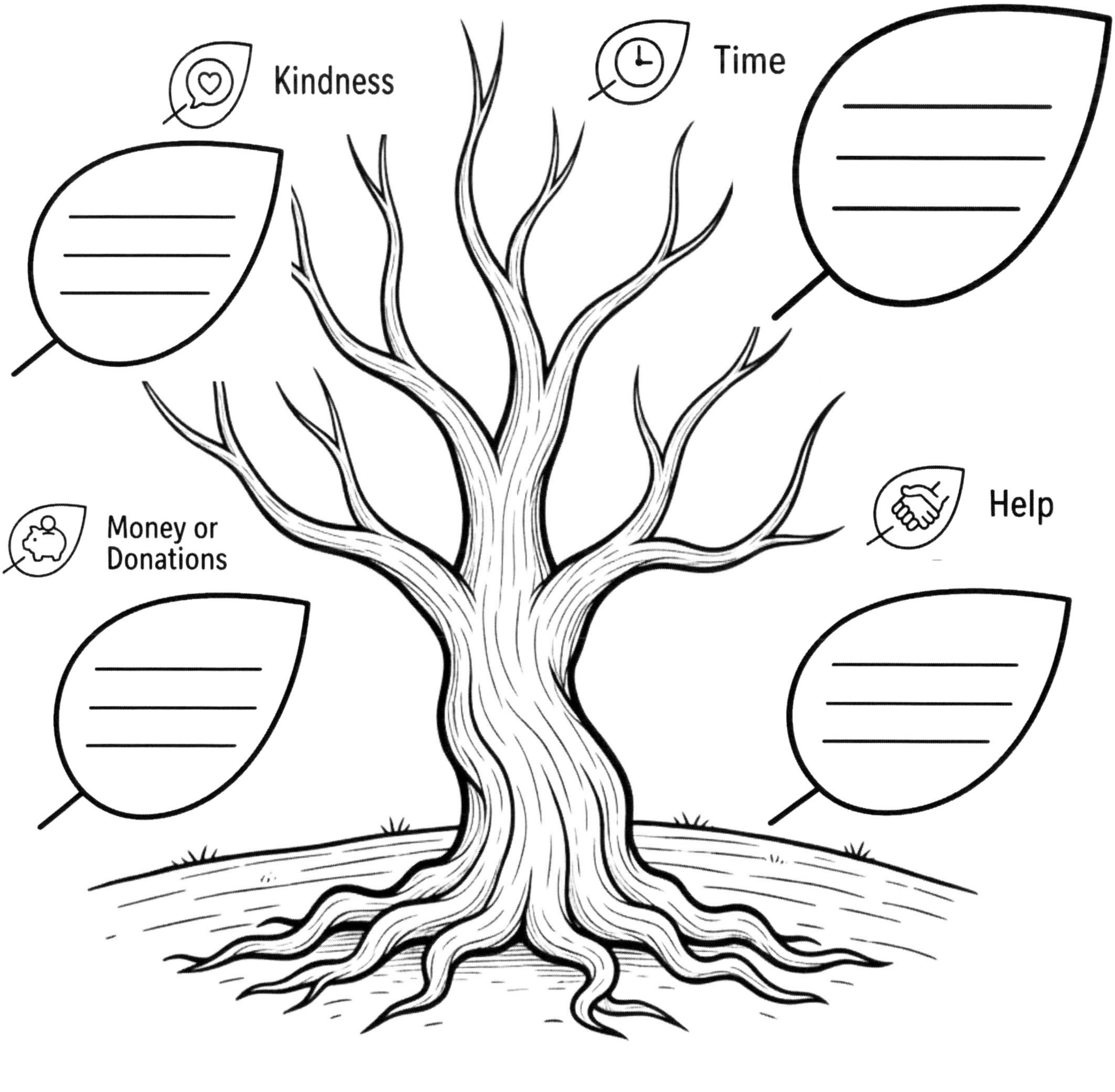

Give, Save, Spend Sorting Game

Theme: Making Smart Money Choices

Instructions:

1. Read the actions below.
2. Draw a line from each action to the jar it belongs to.

Donated $5 to a pet shelter

Bought a toy

Saved $10 in a piggy bank

Gave a classmate lunch money

Bought snacks

Put $2 in a charity box

Donated clothes that no longer fit to a local shelter.

Gave part of my allowance to help plant trees.

Bought art supplies for a class fundraiser.

Put coins in a donation box at the grocery store.

Saved birthday money to buy a new game later.

Put extra change in my savings jar for a school trip.

Added $5 each week toward a new pair of sneakers.

Bought lunch from the school cafeteria.

Paid for movie tickets with friends.

Purchased a small gift for a family member's birthday.

Giving Reflection

Instructions: Reflect on what you have learned in ***The Grove of Giving*** unit. Then answer the questions below.

Curious Questions

What am I still wondering about?

Money I Know

What ideas do I understand now?

My Next Money Moves

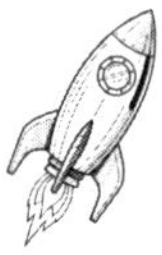

What will I do next?

What three ideas you're ready to take off with?

1.

2.

3.

Answer Keys

Page 7 **Ways to earn money**

Which of these are ways to earn money?

Walking a dog: Yes

Playing video games: No

Selling Lemonade: Yes

Sleeping late: No

Helping with chores: Yes

Watching television: No

Scrolling on social media: No

Cutting the neighbors yard: Yes

Babysitting for neighbors: Yes

Tutoring math: Yes

Page 8 **Finding more ways to earn money**

Earning Money

Q T I M M J L M K T G B S J P I U F L L
I D A W Y E T E Z Y U B E U Q M D Y H R
V T B H K B J T S A K T Q U O A K L J Y
H M C Y H N Y L P R Z H O J A H O T R N
T C A D X C Z D W D X F Q R G M W S L W
C Z E C C C C Q S W M L H G I Q N Q L B
Q J V R A V K O P O T K D T A N Q D G S
N I D Z C H S R N R B I F U M H G D N D
N Y X B C L Q Y W K F Y G C A C C R I N
D G U T A J B G Y I H G L V L G R I L A
J O E T W B H Y R N L N E G L N A P E R
B P G I V R Y R E N O I M N O I F Q V R
J Q D W I K L S V S D P O I W L T H O E
W B Y T A W X Q I B W L N K A C S S H Q
F I G I V L O D L T L E A R N Y E A S N
B J H Y D O K X E J T H D O C C R W I E
H H T J I L I J D J Z I E W E E O R S S
C L E A N I N G P N U Q N Y F R H A V D
T U R N Y V D P U V Z M Y G I F C C O B
D M Q O Z B J G U B I V Z T H M O T M R

1. Chores **2.** Dogwalk **3.** Babysitting **4.** Tutoring **5.** Lemonade **6.** Working

7. Helping **8.** Allowance **9.** Crafts **10.** Recycling **11.** Carwash **12.** Shoveling

13. Yardwork **14.** Errands **15.** Delivery **16.** Cleaning

Earnings

Page 9

Different ways to earn

Page 10

Find 20 Hidden Coins

Bank

In the pediment above the word "BANK"
On the left column
On the right column
On the left door
On the right door
On the left-most step
On the ground in front of the bank
On the window to the left of the doors
On the streetlamp base near the bank

House

Near the roof peak
On the window
On the door
On the chimney
In the tree branches behind the house
In the bush to the right of the house

Grocery Store

On the awning
On the sign to the left of the door
On the door
In the top right corner of the display window
On the roof (top left corner)

Earnings

Page 11

True or False Earning Money Quiz

1. True
2. False
3. True
4. True
5. False
6. True
7. True
8. False (it comes from "pygg" clay pots)
9. True
10. True (in the U.S. and Britain, long ago)
11. False
12. True
13. False
14. True
15. False (it lasts about 5-6 years)
16. True
17. False (it was in 1967 in London)
18. True
19. True
20. False (the U.S. has $2.50, $5, $10, $20 gold coins, and modern $1+ coins)

Page 12

How Long Will It Take

Jack needs to cut **10** yards to reach is goal of $400
It will take Jack **5** weeks to reach his goal, if he cuts two yards per week.

Mia needs to help with laundry **12** times to earn enough for her bike. ($300)
It will take Mia **6** weeks to reach her goal, if she helps twice a each week.

Liam needs to walk **20** dogs to reach is goal of $300.
It will take Liam **5** weeks to reach his goal, if he walks four dogs every week.

Earnings

Page 13

Allan will need to wash **8** cars to buy his headphones. ($120)

It will take Allan **8** weeks to reach his goal, if he washes one car per week.

Rachel needs to help her aunt **10** times to reach her goal. ($300)

It will take Rachel **5** weeks to earn her tablet, If she helps twice a week

Ethan will need to take out the trash **15** times to buy his sneakers ($150) it will take him **5** weeks, If he does this chores three times per week

Page 14

Isaiah's gross pay $1600.00
Isaiah's current deductions $263.40
Isaiah's net pay $1336.60

Page 15

Bessie - Gross Pay = $4,230.77, Deductions = $2,553.00, Net Pay = $1,677.77
Robert - Gross Pay = $3,691.15, Deductions = $2,017.00, Net Pay = $1,674.15

Page 16

Choosing the Right-After School Job for Ruby while Analyzing her Net Earnings

Assume Ruby works a **3-hour shift** each day for all three jobs.

1. **Job A (Retail Clerk)**
   - **Gross Daily Pay**: $18.00/hour x 3 hours = $54.00
   - **Daily Commute Cost**: $9.00
   - **Daily Pay (before taxes)**: $54.00 - $9.00 = $45.00
   - **Hourly Wage**: $45.00 / 3 hours = **$15.00 / hour**

2. **Job B (Library Assistant)**
   - **Gross Daily Pay**: $14.00 / hour x 3 hours = $42.00
   - **Daily Commute Cost**: $0.00
   - **Daily Pay (before taxes)**: $42.00 - $0.00 = $42.00
   - **Hourly Wage**: $42.00 / 3 hours = **$14.00 / hour**

3. **Job C (Tutor)**
   - **Gross Daily Pay**: $16.00 / hour x 3 hours = $48.00
   - **Daily Commute Cost**: $3.00
   - **Daily Pay (before taxes)**: $48.00 - $3.00 = $45.00
   - **Hourly Wage**: $45.00 / 3 hours = **$15.00 / hour**

Ruby should also consider the non-financial trade-offs:

- **Job A**: Offers the highest initial pay, but the **1.5-hour commute** (30% of her working time) means less time for homework or rest.
- **Job B**: Has the lowest pay, but the **15-minute commute** saves her significant time and effort, and there are **no travel costs**.
- ***Job C:*** Offers a Net Hourly Wage equal to Job A, but the **45-minute commute** is much shorter than Job A, making it a strong balance of pay and time.

Now You Decide

Job A pays the most per hour
Job A and Job C cost money to travel to
Job B is the closest to Ruby's home and school
Job C has a strong balance of pay and time

Earnings

Page 17

Helping Gene Choose the Right After-School Job

Gene needs to calculate his **Net Hourly Wage** by factoring in the daily transportation expenses.

Assume Gene works a **2.5-hour shift** each day for all three jobs.

1. Job A (Grocery Store Clerk)
Gross Daily Pay $17.00/hour x 2.5 hours = $42.50
Daily Commute Cost: $6.00
Daily Pay (before taxes): $42.50 - $6.00 = $36.50
Net Hourly Wage $36.50/2.5 hours = $14.60/hour

2. Job B (Dishwasher at Local Diner)
Gross Daily Pay $15.50/hour x 2.5 hours = $38.75
Daily Commute Cost: $0.00
Daily Pay (before taxes): $38.75 - $0.00 = $38.75
Net Hourly Wage $38.75/2.5 hours = $15.50/hour

3. Job C (Community Center Assistant)
Gross Daily Pay $16.50/hour x 2.5 hours = $41.25
Daily Commute Cost: $4.00
Daily Pay (before taxes): $41.25 - $4.00 = $37.25
Net Hourly Wage $37.25/2.5 hours = $14.90/hour

Gene should also consider the non-financial trade-offs:

- **Job A:** Offers a decent gross wage, but the **1-hour commute** and **$6.00 daily cost** significantly reduce his net earnings and free time.
- **Job B:** Although the gross hourly pay is lower, the **short bike ride** means no transportation costs and more time for other activities, resulting in the **highest net hourly wage**.
- **Job C:** A good balance of pay and a manageable commute. His net hourly wage is better than Job A, but slightly less than ***Job B.***

Now You Decide

Job A pays the most per hour
Job A and Job C cost money to travel to
Job B is the closest to Gene's home and school
Job C has a strong balance of pay and time

Page 18

Registered Nurses (RNs) provide and coordinate patient care, educate patients and the public about various health conditions, and offer advice and emotional support to patients and their families.

The following wage estimates are based on **May 2024** data from the BLS:

Statistic	Annual Wage	Hourly Wage
Median Pay	**$93,600**	**$45.00**
Lowest 10%	**$59,450** (May 2021 data)	**$28.58** (May 2021 data)
Highest 10%	**$120,250** (May 2021 data)	**$57.81** (May 2021 data)

Category	Requirement/Detail
Typical Entry-Level Education	**Bachelor's degree** (Bachelor of Science in Nursing - BSN) is common, especially in hospital settings, but entry can also be achieved with an Associate's Degree in Nursing (ADN/ASN) or a diploma from an approved program.
Required	**Nursing License** (must graduate from an approved nursing program and pass a qualifying exam, such as the NCLEX).
Training	Nursing programs include supervised **clinical experience**.
Common Coursework	Anatomy, physiology, microbiology, psychology, and social and behavioral sciences.
Important Skills	**Communication**, **critical thinking** (especially in BSN programs), **leadership** (for administrative roles), and **compassion**.
Advanced Roles	A **Master's degree** is required for advanced practice registered nurses (APRNs) like Nurse Practitioners and Clinical Nurse Specialists (CNSs).

Earnings

Page 20

Massachusetts Pro-Tip - The 18/65 Law (M.G.L. c. 167D, s. 5): Under MA state law, state-chartered banks **must** offer a "18/65 Account" to anyone 18 or under or older than 65. These accounts are special because they have **no monthly fees** and **no minimum balance requirements**, and **offer free basic check orders**. Always ask the banker for the "18/65" option!

Lastly: Always check the "fine print." While The 18/65 Law covers most things, banks may still charge fees for "extra" services like out-of-network ATMs, wire transfers, or replacing a lost debit card. (Note: Under this law, any "Insufficient Funds" or overdraft fee is legally capped at $5.00).

Page 21

Banking Knowledge

Balance	How much money you have right now.
Debit Card	A card that lets you spend your own money in your checking account.
Withdrawal	Taking money *out* of your account.
Interest	Money the bank pays you for keeping your money there.
Deposit	Putting money *into* your bank account.
Direct Deposit	Your paycheck goes straight into your bank account.
Credit Union	A bank-like place where people who are members join together to save money and borrow money. It is owned by the members, not by a company.
PIN	A secret number used to keep your debit card safe.
Fee	Money the bank charges for certain services (like overdrafting or using another bank's ATM).
Overdraft	When you spend more money than you have in your account.
Statement	A monthly record that shows how much money was spent and saved.
Mobile Banking	Using a smartphone or device to conduct financial transactions through a bank's app or website.

Savings

Page 24

Savings Word Match

Piggy Bank	Something you are saving money for, like a bike, game, or trip.
Interest	A plan for how you will spend and save your money.
Goal	Extra money you earn from the bank for keeping your savings there.
Deposit	A safe place (like a jar or little bank) where you put your money to save.
Budget	Putting money into a bank account or savings spot.

Savings Scramble

SNOIC: <u>COINS</u>

CUNTOAC: <u>ACCOUNT</u>

EFAS: <u>SAFE</u>

GVISSNA: <u>SAVINGS</u>

AKNB: <u>BANK</u>

Page 25 **Quiz: True or False**

1. T
2. F
3. T

Game: "Savings Race"

Answer: 10 Weeks

Page 26-27

Savings Crossword

Across

5. WITHDRAW
6. EMERGENCY
10. ALLOWANCE
11. NEED
12. DEPOSIT
13. TRACK
15. PIGGYBANK

Down

1. SPENDING
2. BUDGET
3. SAVE
4. PLAN
7. GOAL
8. BANK
9. INTEREST
14. ACCOUNT

Page 28

Decoded Message

Do not save what is left after spending; instead, spend what is left after saving.

Page 29

Riddle: *I'm where every dollar goes, that's the plan.*
I stop your money from slipping away,
and help your savings grow each day.
Answer: budget

Page 30

Nature's Savers

Squirrels (e)
Beavers (a)
Ants (f)
Woodpeckers (b)
Honey Bees (c)
Hamsters (d)

"That's it, Pugsley! We're finished with the **Savings** section. Let's move on to the **Spending** section."

Great, Clover, let's go.

Spending

Page 32	**Needs** vs	**Wants**
	Water Fruit (Food) Housing School Supplies	Candy Gaming Console Toys Ice Cream Movie (Tickets) Shoes may be a need, but designer shoes are a want
Page 34	**Smart Shopping**	Vanessa's Answer: B $56 Noah's Answer: B $96
Page 35	**Smart Shopping**	Reggie's Answer: Both are $30 Jasmine"s Answer: A $50
Page 36	**Budget Plan**	20% = $40 15% = $30 15% = $30 15% = $30 10% = $20 15% = $30 10% = $20
Page 43	**Jasmine's Spending Budget Pie**	Jasmine's **Spending** slice is the biggest. A teenager's spending would generally be the largest because they often have numerous personal desires and social activities that require money.

If Jasmine needed or wanted to grow her **"Savings"** slice, here are a few things she can do:

Get a job or side hustle: She can earn more money through part-time work, freelancing, or chores.
Create a budget: She should track her income and expenses to identify areas to cut back.
Reduce unnecessary spending: She can cut down on non-essential purchases like daily snacks, impulse buys, or excessive entertainment.
Set clear savings goals: Jasmine can set a specific target, such as saving for a phone, a concert, or college, to provide motivation.
Automate savings: She can set up a regular transfer of a portion of her income directly into a savings account.

If Jasmine's 'Spending' slice kept getting bigger, her savings would **decrease** until they eventually reached **zero**.

Spending

Pages 45-46

Jasmine's budgeting story

Budget
Gross Pay
Deductions
Net Pay
Income
Fixed Expenses
Variable Expenses
Needs
Disposable Income
Allocation
Discretionary Spending
Wants
Expenses
Cost of Living
Emergency Fund
Savings
Assets
Liabilities
Cash Flow
Budget

Page 48

Clover's Technology Upgrade vs. Old Technology

Part 1: Mathematical Analysis

1. **Option A (Newest Model):** $1,200 /5 years = $240
2. **Option B (Refurbished Model):** $600 /3 years = $200
3. **Option C (Repair):** $150 /1 year = $150

Reflection: Based solely on the Annual Cost, which option is the most financially efficient? Answer: Option C

Page 49

Part 2: **Trade-Off Scenario**

If Clover chooses **Option A ($1,200)**, she will have ___**0**___ left in her savings?

The primary risk of Clover spending all of her savings on a new laptop is that she will have no money left for unexpected expenses or emergencies.

The non-financial risk for Clover choosing to repair her old laptop instead of buying a new one is the potential for continued or recurring technical issues, unreliability, and slower performance, which could disrupt her work, studies, or daily tasks.

As Clover, if I knew I had another year of school after this one, I would likely choose to **repair the old laptop (Option C)**, provided the repair cost is reasonable and it offers a good chance of stable performance for the remaining year.

Here's why:

Cost-Effectiveness for Short-Term Need: A new laptop is a significant investment. For just one more year of school, a repair is almost certainly the most cost-effective solution, allowing Clover (or me) to save a substantial amount of money compared to buying a new one.

Part 3: Research and Fill-in-the-Blank

1. Depreciation.
2. Opportunity cost.
3. Refurbished

Spending

Page 50

Randy's The End-of-Year Trip Decision: France vs. Spain

Part 1: Trip Cost Comparison

Cost Category	Trip to France	Trip to Spain
Package Price	$2,200	$1,800
Nights Hotel	$0	$600 ($150x4 nights)
Local Transportation	$0	$175 ($25 x 7 days)
Required Tip/Insurance Fee	$100	$75
Meals (Lunches & Dinners)	$350 ($50x7 days)	$315 ($45 x 7 days)
Total Out-of-Pocket Costs	**A. $450**	**B. $1,165**

Page 51

Part 2: Mathematical Analysis

1. **Total Cost France (Trip A):** $2,200 + $450 = $2,650
2. **Total Cost Spain (Trip B):** $1,800 + $1,165 = $2,965
3. **Final Comparison:** Answer: The trip to **France**

The Lesson Learned

The trip to France, though initially costing $400 more in the package price ($2,200 vs $1,800), end up being $315 cheaper overall ($2,650 vs $2,965) because it includes expensive necessities like lodging and transportation.

Page 52

Mathematical Analysis

1. Option A **Loan Amount**: $22,000 - $4,000 = 1. $18,000
2. Option B **Loan Amount**: $12,000 - $4,000 = 2. $8,000

Page 53

Total Cost of Ownership (TCO) Calculation

Subtotal Monthly Payment 3. $759.63 4. $647.01

Total Annual Expense

3. Option A Monthly Cost: Sum of all monthly costs = 3. $ 759.63
4. Option B Monthly Cost: Sum of all monthly costs = 4. $ 647.01
5. Option A Total Annual TCO: $759.63 x 12 months = 5. $9,115.56
6. Option B Total Annual TCO: $647.01 x 12 months = 6. $7,764.12

TCO Analysis: **Option B** has the lower Total Cost of Ownership

Reflection, Decision, and Discussion Questions

Instructions: Use the financial results and common knowledge to answer the following questions.

1. Which car has a lower Total Cost of Ownership (TCO) in the first year? **Option B (Used Compact)**

2. **Debt and Interest:** Which car carries a higher total cost due to **interest?** Based on the *loan amount* and *term*, Option A (New Sedan) is likely to carry a higher total cost due to interest, even with a lower interest rate, because the principal borrowed ($18,000) is significantly higher and the loan term (5 years) is longer.
   - *(To get a precise total interest paid, one would need to calculate the amortization for both loans. However, given the options, the higher principal and longer term of Option A will almost certainly result in more total interest paid.)*

3. **Depreciation:** What is **depreciation?** Depreciation is the decrease in value of an asset (like a car) over time due to wear and tear, age, and obsolescence.
   - **Why does buying a used car usually mean you suffer less from the effects of depreciation than buying a new car?** New cars depreciate the most rapidly during their first few years of ownership (losing approximately 20-30% of their value in the first year alone, and up to 50% or more within three to five years). When you buy a used car, someone else has already absorbed the steepest part of that depreciation curve. Therefore, the car you buy has already lost a significant portion of its value, and its future depreciation will be at a slower rate, meaning you lose less money to depreciation during your ownership period.

4. **Final Decision:** If your monthly budget for transportation can't exceed $500, which car is the only responsible choice? Explain your reasoning using the calculated Subtotal Monthly Payment. Answer: The only responsible choice would be **neither car** if the *total monthly transportation budget* (which includes more than just the loan payment) cannot exceed $500.

Reasoning:

- Option A's Subtotal Monthly Payment is $759.63, which already exceeds the $500 budget *before* adding other essential transportation costs like insurance, fuel, maintenance, and registration.
- Option B's Subtotal Monthly Payment is $647.01, which also exceeds the $500 budget *before* adding other essential transportation costs.

Therefore, given the strict $500 monthly transportation budget, Antonio would need to reconsider both options as presented, or find a less expensive vehicle/loan option to stay within his budget.

Page 55

Fill in the blanks

Bank (Savings)
Stock
Business
Invest
Profit
Assets
Income
Risk
Value
Compound
Dividend
Budget

Page 56

The Wealth Garden Challenge

(1) Risk Weed
(2) Savings Plant
(3) Profit Tree
(4) Investment Vine
(5) Dividend Flower
(6) Compound Interest Tree

Page 57

Seed or Weed?

Packing your lunch	Seed
Buying Video games	Weed
Saving for a bike	Seed
Buying snacks	Weed
Doing chores	Seed

Page 58

Snake or Safe?

Spending all your allowance on snacks	
Buying matching shoes when you don't have enough money	
Comparing prices and saving $30	✓
Getting tricked online and losing $50	
Writing down your savings goal and sticking to your plan.	✓
Borrowing $20 from a friend and forgetting to pay them back	
Waiting a week before buying something to see if you still want it	✓

Notes:

Giving

Page 68

The Giving Grove Maze

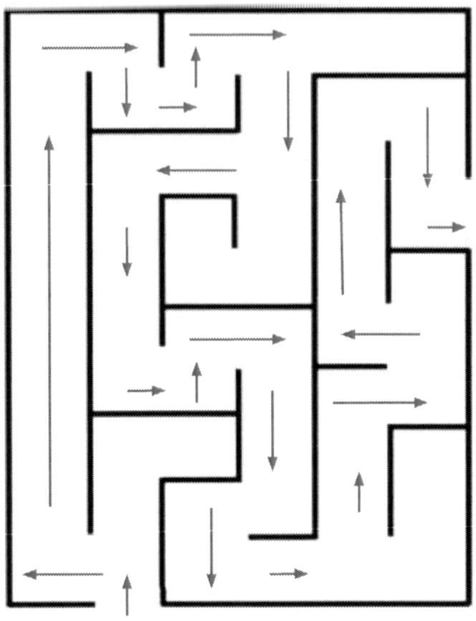

Page 69

Scrambler

Kindness

Charity

Service

Generosity

Donation

Sharing

Contribution

Empathy

Altruism

Compassion

Philanthropy

Gift

Page 70

Pugsley's Giving Phrase Of The Day

SHARING IS CARING

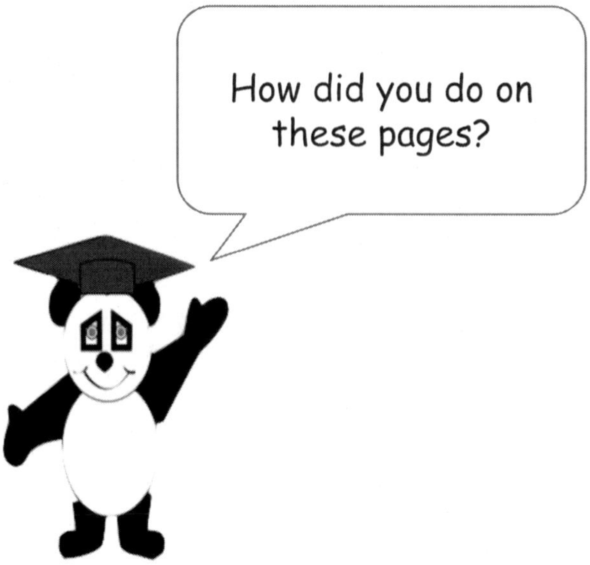

Page 72 Give, Save, Spend Sorting Game

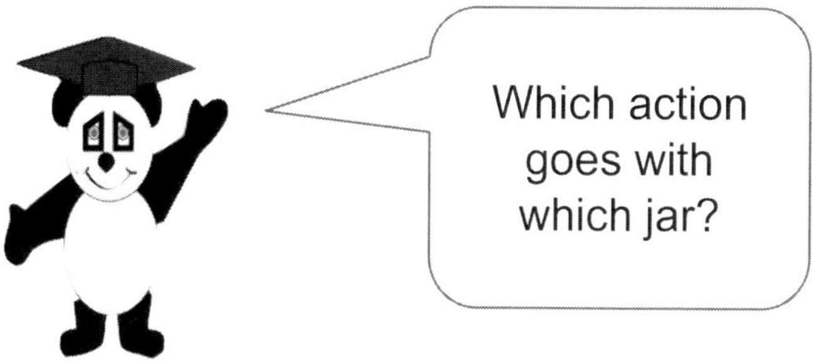

Donated $5 to a pet shelter

Bought a toy

Saved $10 in a piggy bank

Gave a classmate lunch money

Bought snacks

Put $2 in a charity box

Donated clothes that no longer fit to a local shelter.

Gave part of my allowance to help plant trees.

Bought art supplies for a class fundraiser.

Put coins in a donation box at the grocery store.

Saved birthday money to buy a new game later.

Put extra change in my savings jar for a school trip.

Added $5 each week toward a new pair of sneakers.

Bought lunch from the school cafeteria.

Paid for movie tickets with friends.

Purchased a small gift for a family member's birthday.

Explore the Playground Education Collection

The Money Compass Series

The Playground Project

Featuring

Business Bob, Giving Gwen, Math Mary, and Time Terrence

A creative exploration of entrepreneurship and business basics designed to turn your big ideas into reality.

Your Essential Guide to Earning, Budgeting, Investing, and Thriving in Your Teens and Beyond

Featuring

Business Bob, Math Mary, and Time Terrence

Master the leap into adulthood with expert strategies for landing your first professional job, building a bulletproof budget, and using the "Savings Shield" to stay debt-free and financially secure.

Road To Independence

Featuring

Business Bob, Geography Gerald, History Hope, Math Mary, Safety Sam, and Science Scott

Master the milestones of adulthood by learning how to build a powerful credit score, navigate the world of renting and home buying, and choose between leasing or buying your first vehicle—all while staying protected from modern financial scams.

Pugsley Panda

Clover

Also Available from Playground Education

"No Bullying"
Featuring
Safety Sam

"Wellington Hill Playground"
Featuring
The Educational Kidz

"Famous Landmarks in The United States"
Featuring
Geography Gerald

"Children's Safety Tips" - For All Seasons
Featuring
Safety Sam

"How Does Water Recycle"
Featuring
Science Scott

"Character Counts" - Part I
Featuring
Politeness Petunia & Kindness Karl

"Character Counts" - Part II
Featuring
Politeness Petunia & Kindness Karl

THE EDUCATIONAL PANDA

©

PUGSLEY PANDA

Made in United States
North Haven, CT
05 November 2026

21765283R00052